My Story

AN ARTIST JOURNEY

FROM ashes TO BEAUTY

SERENO

Sandy Sereno

Balboa Press books may be ordered through booksellers or by contacting:

Balboa Press
A Division of Hay House
1663 Liberty Drive
Bloomington, IN 47403
www.balboapress.com
1 (877) 407-4847

Library of Congress Control Number: 2019900454

ISBN: 978-1-9822-1714-3 (sc)
ISBN: 978-1-9822-1713-6 (e)

Print information available on the last page.

Balboa Press rev. date: 02/20/2019

Balboa
PRESS
A DIVISION OF HAY HOUSE

Tears Flow down
My Face
My Uncle wanted
sexual favors
from me at age
seven!!! Paid
ME for takeing core of his
needs!!!
FEIT Dirty, ugly, unworthy
of love!!! FEIT I didn't
deserve to be for
prosperous
Money Represente
dirtyness to me
so for most of my
life I remained unworth
Poor!!!...of love,

Sereno ©

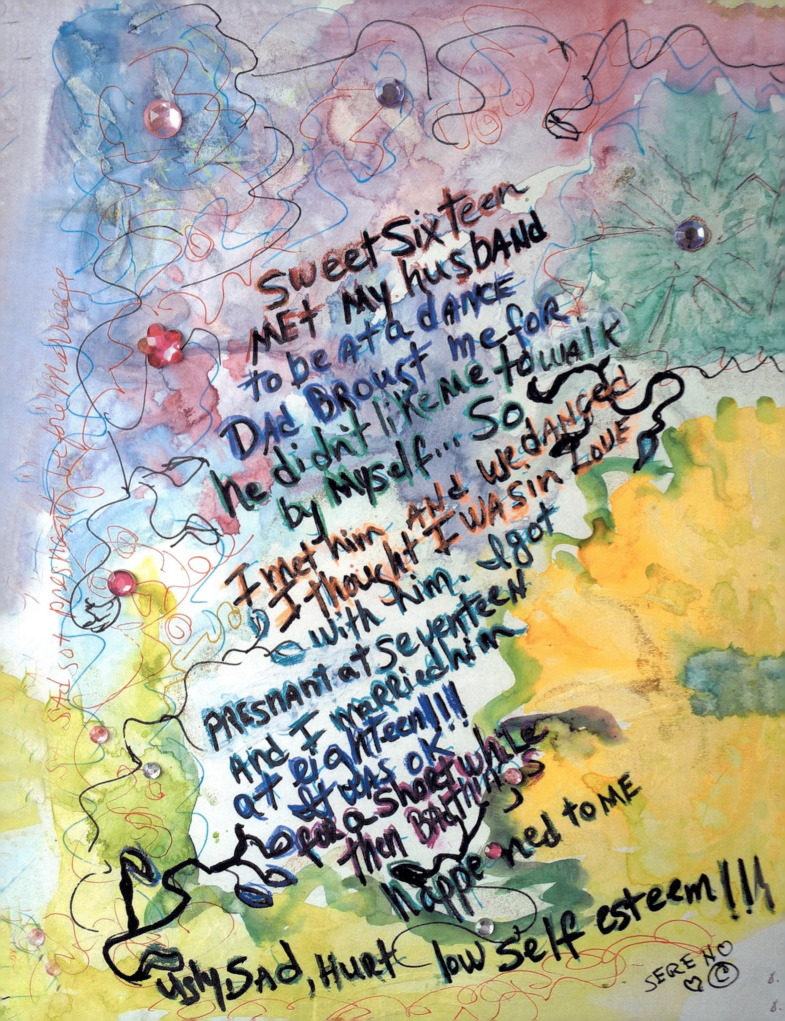

Sweet Sixteen
met my husband
to be at a dance
Dad brought me for
he didn't like me to walk
by myself... So
I met him and we danced
I thought I was in love
with him. I got
presnant at seventeen
and I married him
at eighteen!!!
It was ok
for a short while
then Brathalys
happened to me

ugly Sad, Hurt low self esteem!!!

SERENO

I WAS MARRIED briefly to my husband...
He surpeised Me by being MEAN to ME.
He would verbally abuse ME and
sometimes physically as well...
We would go to visit his grandma
And he would get Angry with me
And LEAVE ME stranded at his
grandmother's house Thirty
miles Away from home...
Eight months pregnat with my W
baby girl he would so... Hi sure
had to drive ME home... Then he wou
accuse ME of being with his uncle...
Last thing on my mind being 8 months
pregnant... I had long hair and sometime
he would pull it... one time he pulled
My hair outdoors And wanted to
Run over ME with his car... New
Year's Day I left him with my 2 babies
I left him, Divorced him at age 20

It took courage to leave this man at 20 years old...
But I did it

Daughter Sheila
Son DARcy

SERENO
♡ ☺ Courageous Strong
Hurt Ugly
Shamed Unloved

ABUSED
USED

2. It WAS. A terrible experience

ONE Night
I DECIDED to go
out to a club

I WAS 21 years young
NIEVE About MEN
I had A few drinks
And went with a guy
a stranger... Went to
his Apartment don't
Remember All the details
But he proceeded to strangle
ME... I BEGGED him to let
ME go... But he continued to
STRANGLE ME... he let ME go
And Raped ME from Behind
HE placed his Rod in my fanny
as soon as HE WAS done he let
ME go... NO UEHICIE SO I Ran
And Ran All the WAY Home...
didn't tell A SouL kept it inside
of ME... NEVER looked At my
throat until it healed
I forgot About incident
until I WAS 67 years young
That story is told at the
end of this book

RAGE TERROR death HORROR

12.

The Looking Glass

21

used here

hot balding

ugly old

Rejected oh! oh! oh!

I met this MAN at a club. I was 21 years young very naive about MEN I went with him to my home we made love... Went to see him the next evening at club... All his friends AND him laughed at me or so I thought... I ran home went to bathroom AND said I was ugly going bald for I cut my hair short...

SERENO ©©

And there I stayed blocked until I was in my...

SERENO ©©

down I went again to the Bottom of the sea!!!

I Met A FIREMAN AT A club... He was so cute... I thought he was my TWIN FLAME... I fell IN LOVE with him... ONE night he called me to come over to his home I went and later his girlfriend came over... We got into a fight... she kept pounding my head... she WAS Angry, finally he got her off of me And told her he didn't call me. He pulled my hair And tossed me out the door

Some years later I saw him he Apologized And moved to the country. He wanted to be with me. Now that he was drug-free and clean, I told him no, one incident WAS enough!!

Abused

Scared

DEVASTATED

SERENE

AGE OF AQUARIOUS
HIPPY DAYS

Joins with other hippies

WHEN THE MOON
collides with
the sun This
is the AGE OF Aquarious

Happy
Fun Love
Camping

I HAD 2 children
felt Loved my x-husband...A boy
And a girl...Early...18-19 years
young...I joined
THE Hippy
Movement
around 25 years
young...It was
fun went to the
White Mountains of NH where
a lot of us Hippies Camped out
I went with a
few MEN And I
got PRESNANT
with my 3rd
girl I called
her
Crystal

Joy...A Sereno Fort

sweet

Love

SEREN

The Crystal
Visions
'18

THE AGE OF AQUARIOUS
My Hippy Days

I MET my 3rd childs father at
the WHITE Mountains of NEW
Hampshire... I became pregnat
with my daughter Crystal...
HER father came home with me
And we liVED together for a few
months... I let him use my van
to go find a job... while I walked
to work 6 months pregnant...
Later on I found out that he
was meeting other girls with my
van... instead of getting work...
I then told him he needed to
leave for I wasn't going to
support him and three
children... nor did I want
someone to cheat on me
either... so he left and
never saw his baby or
called or any-thing...

Sereno ©

so sad felt lost lonely rejected
very hurt puzzled

20.

The Mountain Man

I Met This man in my Hippy Days... He was married at that time... I met him in the White Mts of New Hampshire when I was twenty-five We Ran into each other throughout the years but he was still married... didn't go with him at that time... Around fifty years young I ReMet him at a Restaurant told me his wife died... That was sad... I went out with him off and on for several years... I wasn't in Love with him and he Really wasn't in Love with me... It was a Relationship of convenience... He didn't like taking me out, nor hardly bought me any gifts... When I went to his home, it was all about him, no kissing, didn't please me in anyway... So we parted ways that was over 10 years ago... No Relationship since..

THE KISS

When I Turned 67 years young, I went to Live in Florida for the winter (I Live in my VAN). It would be very cold in New Hampshire during the winter. One day I prayed to God and asked him to send me a new husband.... A day or two later as I was sitting in McDonald's on my laptop in Bradenton Florida in walked this man with a big sombrero on his head and a Knapsack on his back... He took off his hat And he was bald (hum I don't like bald headed men). I thought he was a street person. He sat way across me, facing me so he could watch me. He kept staring at me across the Room... Later he walked towards me. And said his name was Jacob... Oh !!! he has a biblical name (coincidence). I don't like bald headed men... He invited me to his RV, of course I still thought he was a street person... He kept coming to McDonald's and a few other places nearby that I was at. He continued to invite me to his RV, finally I went and he has this big motorhome.... So, he's not a street person.. I went in his RV, we talk, had wine And he kissed me near my right shoulder. Even though he is bald, he is very handsome. I started to like him a lot... Time stood still, one moment it was light out, the next moment it was dark...

He left for a while but during that time unusual occurrences started happening. I started to remember all the hurts, pain, abuses and men who used during my life... I had forgotten all these incidents, that were locked within my heart...

THE KISS Awakened all those Repressed memories that resided in my Heart... Unknown to me. I cried, walked, cried some more, hit sticks And Released all those old memories... And pain within my Heart.. My Heart is Now free And I Now feel so BEAutiful for I Thought

I AM Grateful that God sent me this MAN to help me unlock the old memories from my heart

I feel so much love in my heart!!

I was so ugly Another Repressed memory.

IF I kiss The Frog King
What do you think will happen?
Will he stay a Frog King?
If I kiss the Frog King with
Love, kindness and gentleness,
Will this handsome Frog King that's
perched in my Right hand change
into my King?
If I tell him I Love I Love
him with all my Heart and soul
will he turn into my handsome MAN
My twin FLAME, the
other part of my soul.
My Love who has been my
soul mate since the
beginning of time.
It is time for us to
Merge as one once
again for all
Eternity

Serena ♥ ©

30.

The Hidden Secrets of My Heart

From Ashes to Beauty

My Heart was cleansed by my Tears
and Many Hurts, pain And abuses
were washed away... A lot of anger
was also realeased during this time
which was still in my Heart
at the young age of 67...

I thought I was ugly,
unloved and undeserving of
love from a wonderful
man, I carried all of these
incidents inside my
Heart for many
years all locked
away And I must
have thrown away the key...

I was never truly LOVED
By any MAN throughout my
life even now at the young
Age of 68...

Now that most of these
memories are released
I feel so Beautiful
full of Life And vitality
I'M Now Ready to Begin a
New And Better Life for myself,
as a woman and an Artist...
Ready to pursue My DREAMS
I'VE BEEN SET FREE
TO BE ME!!!
BEAUTIFUL AND LOVED
I AM Truly Grateful
TO GOD AND Goddess
for My New
LIFE

SERENA

The King

I Know Now that I Deserve to be LOVED like I never Known Before!!!

I Embrace the LOVE in my HEART AS I open The Petals that have been closed Oh these many years... Each Petal grows with more LOVE... I Look forward to EMBRACE My King My ONE True LOVE I AWAIT FOR MY KING to ARRIVE IN MY LIFE I Deserve TRUE LOVE And so do you all!!!

I LOVE you All for Being on My JOURNEY with me in this BOOK!!!

THANK YOU

SERENO ♥

Let your Heart Guide You

create celebrate

Follow your dreams you were born to BE

create with all your HEART

You Are A MESSAGE

HAVE COURAGE to be You!!!

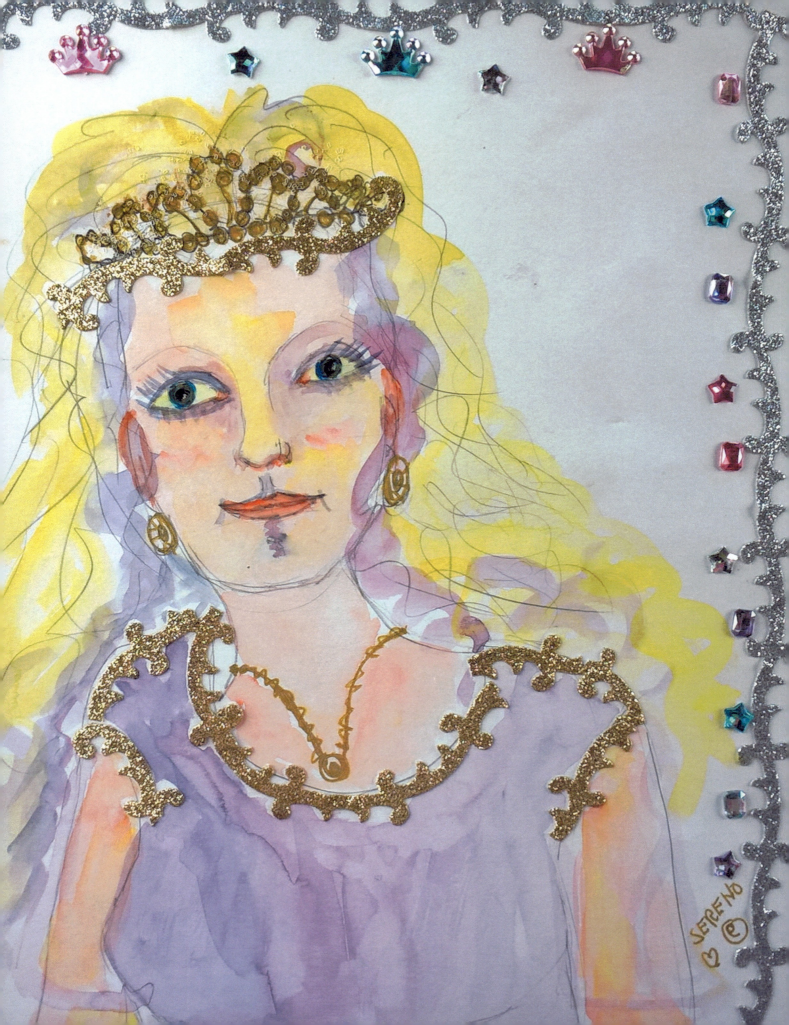

MY SECRET DESIRES OF MY HEART

NOW I Truly feel Like a QUEEN BEAUTIFUL and wonderfully Made by the CREATOR of the Universe.

MY HEART IS NOW OPEN to RECEIVE MANY Blessings from the Universe

My Desires of My Heart

1. To GET MARRIED to a wonderful, loving MAN
2. To have a Home filled with LOVE AND LIGHT. (for I Live in my VAN)
3. To be a rich, prosperous And successful ARTiST.
4. To have BEAUTiful Long Thick strong Hair

This is my petition to the Universe

MY NEW Adventures are NOW BEGINNING!!!

The NEW story of My Life!!!

This is the BEGINNING of my life!!!

LOVE is in The Air

SERE 40

Printed in the United States
By Bookmasters